Nick Vandome

Get going with

Windows 10

in
easy steps

In easy steps is an imprint of In Easy Steps Limited
16 Hamilton Terrace · Holly Walk · Leamington Spa
Warwickshire · United Kingdom · CV32 4LY
www.ineasysteps.com

Notice of Liability
Every effort has been made to ensure that this book contains accurate and
current information. However, In Easy Steps Limited and the author shall not be
liable for any loss or damage suffered by readers as a result of any information
contained herein. All prices stated in the book are correct at the time of printing.

Trademarks
All trademarks are acknowledged as belonging to their respective companies.

In Easy Steps Limited supports The Forest Stewardship Council (FSC), the leading
international forest certification organisation. All our titles that are printed on
Greenpeace approved FSC certified paper carry the FSC logo.

MIX
Paper from
responsible sources
FSC® C020837

Printed and bound in the United Kingdom·
ISBN 978-1-84078-684-2

Contents

1 Introducing Windows 10

Windows 10 provides a return to a more familiar
look and feel for Windows users, particularly on
desktop and laptop computers with a mouse and
keyboard. This chapter details the new features
in Windows 10, including the new web browser,
Microsoft Edge, and the personal voice assistant,
Cortana, but also the ways in which it has reinstated
some of the more traditional items, such as the
Start Menu.

Windows 10: the Next Step

All major computer operating systems (OS) undergo regular upgrades and new versions. Sometimes these are a significant visual overhaul, while others concentrate more on the behind-the-scenes aspect of the OS. In the terms of Windows, Windows 8 was one of the most radical updates to the User Interface (UI) and introduced a number of new features, for both desktop and mobile versions of Windows. However, it was not met with universal approval, as it was perceived that it was two separate operating systems (desktop and mobile) bolted together, whilst not satisfying each environment completely.

With Windows 10, a lot of the problems with Windows 8 have been addressed: the familiar Start Menu has been reinstated to return to a similar UI to earlier versions of Windows; there has been greater consolidation between desktop and mobile devices running Windows 10; and the operation of apps has been standardized so that it is similar for both the new Windows apps, and also the more traditional ones. In a sense, this is a case of going back one step in order to go forwards two steps and Windows 10 has succeeded in creating a familiar environment, coupled with a range of new features.

New features

In addition to the return to familiar ground are a number of new features, including a new web browser, Microsoft Edge, that allows users to draw on and annotate web pages and then send them to other people.

There is also a new personal digital assistant and voice search, Cortana, to help elevate Windows 10 to be the most advanced operating system that Microsoft has produced.

It is free to upgrade to Windows 10 from Windows 7, 8 or 8.1 (not Enterprise editions) but for earlier versions, e.g. Windows Vista and XP, a DVD is required for undertaking a clean installation, which does not save settings or files so these will need to be backed up prior to installation.

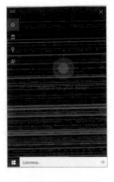

Tapping and swiping gestures can be used for touchscreen devices with Windows 10 but one of its aims is to make it more familiar again for mouse and keyboard users.

Don't forget

Getting a Microsoft Account

A Microsoft Account is required for many of the features of Windows 10. It is free to create and can be done with an email address and, together with a password, this provides a unique identifier for logging into your Microsoft Account and the related apps. There are several ways in which you can create and set up a Microsoft Account:

- During the initial setup process when you install Windows 10. You will be asked if you want to create a Microsoft Account at this point. If you do not, you can always do so at a later time.

- When you first open an app that requires access to a Microsoft Account. When you do this you will be prompted to create a new account.

- From the **Accounts** section of the **Settings** app.

Whichever way you use to create a Microsoft Account the process is similar:

1 When you are first prompted to sign in with a Microsoft Account you can enter your account details, if you have one, or

2 Click on the **No account? Create one!** link

No account? Create one!

3 Enter your name, an email address and a password for your Microsoft Account

Let's create your account

Windows, Office, Outlook.com, OneDrive, Skype, Xbox. They're all better and more personal when you sign in with your Microsoft account.* Learn more

Nick | Vandome

✔ After you sign up, we'll send you a message with a link to verify this user name.

nickvandome2@gmail.com
Get a new email address

••••••••

United States

Birth month ✕ | Day ✕ | Year ✕

Back | Next

4 Click on the **Next** button to move through the registration process

Next

5 Enter your password again to confirm your account

6 Click on the **Finish** button in the final window to complete setting up your Microsoft Account

Make it yours

Windows is better when your settings and files automatically sync. If you make nickvandome2@gmail.com your primary account, Windows will use it

To make nickvandome2@gmail.com your primary account, we'll need your Windows password one last time to make sure it's really you.

Your Windows password

I'll connect my Microsoft account later.

Next

Start Button and Start Menu

One of the main criticisms of Windows 8 was the redesign of the Start Button and the Start Screen. This was incorporated into a pane that filled the screen and, by default, appeared whenever the computer was turned on. In Windows 10, Microsoft has gone backwards, in some ways, in order to move forward. The Start Button and Start Menu that are familiar in operation to Windows 7 users, and earlier, have been reinstated. However, the Start Menu has also been redesigned to incorporate some of the best features of the Windows 8 Start Screen.

Start Button

The Start Button is available in the bottom, left-hand corner of the screen and this is used to access the Start Menu.

The Start Menu can also be accessed from the Windows button (WinKey) on the keyboard.

There is also a contextual menu that can be accessed by right-clicking on the Start Button. This contains links to items such as the Control Panel, File Explorer and the Task Manager.

Start Menu

Many Windows users were aghast when the Start Menu disappeared in Windows 8. This was the list of links and frequently used apps that enabled users to move around areas of their computer. In Windows 8 this was replaced by a full-screen format of colored tiles, known as the Start Screen. In Windows 10 the Start Menu has been reinstated, including some of the better elements of the Start Screen. The Start Menu consists of shortcuts to regularly used items, such as All apps and Settings, frequently used apps and an area where tiles can be added for accessing apps and also viewing live information within them:

User account icon   Start Menu tiles

Shortcut links   Most used apps

Click on your own account icon to access options for changing your account settings, locking your session, or signing out of your account.

Settings and Control Panel

Windows 8.1 introduced a new Settings app for customizing the way that your computer looks and operates. This has been continued with Windows 10. However, the familiar Control Panel can now be used to specify some of the same settings and also some different ones.

Settings

The Settings app can be accessed from the Start Menu:

1 Click on the Start Button

2 Click on the **Settings** button on the Start Menu, or the **Settings** tile on the Start Screen

3 The Settings are displayed under nine main categories

4 Click on a category to view the items within it

...cont'd

Control Panel
The traditional Windows Control Panel can also be used to customize
your computer, although it can be slightly harder to find initially:

1 Right-click on the Start Button and click on the
Control Panel button, or

2 Click on the Start Button and click on the **All apps** button

3 Scroll through the apps. Click on
Windows System > Control Panel

4 The familiar
Control Panel
opens at its
Homepage

When accessing the Control Panel in Step 3,
right-click on it and select **Pin to Start** or
Pin to taskbar to pin it to these areas,
for quick access.

Signing In

When you sign in to your account from the Lock Screen, you can specify what to enter in terms of a password, PIN number or a picture password. To do this:

1 Access the **Accounts** category within **Settings**

2 Click on the **Sign-in options** button in the left-hand panel

3 Click on the **Add** button next to a sign-in method to create it (or **Change** for an existing one)

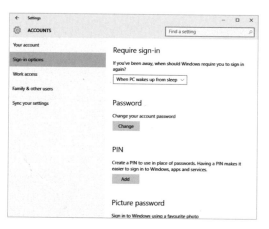

4 For the **Picture password** option you can choose a picture and then specify a gesture that has to be applied to it to unlock your account

2 Start Button and Menu

This chapter shows how to use the Start Button and also the improved Start Menu, which has returned to Windows after being removed in Windows 8 and 8.1. The elements of the Start Menu are explained and there are also details about how your favorite apps can be pinned to the Start Menu so that they can be accessed quickly.

Start Button

When the predecessor to Windows 10 (Windows 8) was introduced
there was a significant outcry due to the disappearance of the traditional
Windows Start Button. This was made worse by the removal of the
Start Menu too. However, the Start Button was reinstated in Windows
8.1 and the Start Menu has now also returned, in an enhanced format.
This means that Windows 10 can be used in a similar way to traditional
versions of Windows.

Using the Start Button

The Start Button provides access to the apps on your Windows 10 PC
and also the enhanced Start Menu:

1   Click on the **Start Button** in the bottom
left-hand corner of the screen

2   The **Start Menu** is displayed. The
left-hand side can be used to access
apps from various locations

3 The right-hand side of the **Start Menu** is where apps can be pinned so that they are always available. This is displayed as a collection of large, colored tiles

4 Other items can also be accessed from the **Start Button** by right-clicking on it

Programs and Features
Mobility Center
Power Options
Event Viewer
System
Device Manager
Network Connections
Disk Management
Computer Management
Command Prompt
Command Prompt (Admin)

Task Manager
Control Panel
File Explorer
Search
Run

Shut down or sign out
Desktop

Click on the **Power** button on the Start Menu to specify actions to be taken when you press your computer's power button.

Hot tip

Start Menu

The reinstated Start Menu in Windows 10 is where you can access areas within your computer, perform certain functions and also access apps from a variety of locations.

1 Click here to access your own account settings or sign out from your account

2 Click here to access the **File Explorer**, your **Documents** library within File Explorer and the Windows 10 **Settings**

3 Your most frequently used apps are displayed here. Click on one to open it (these items will change as you use different apps)

4 Click on the **Power** button (or right-click on the Start Button) for options to **Sleep** your computer, **Shut down** or **Restart**

5 Click on the **All apps** button to access a list of all of the apps on your computer. Use the scroll bar at the right-hand side to move through the list of apps (see pages 62-63)

6 Click on the **Back** button return to the Start Menu view

7 If there is a down-pointing arrow next to an app this means that there are additional items that can be accessed. Click on the arrow to view these

Hot tip

The items that appear on the Start Menu can be customized within **Settings > Personalization > Start**.

19

Pinning Apps

The apps that you use most frequently can be pinned to the Start Menu (or Taskbar) for quick access. To do this:

1 Click on the **All apps** button on the Start Menu to access a list of your apps

2 Right-click on the app that you want to pin to the Start Menu and click on **Pin to Start** (or **Pin to taskbar** to pin the app to the Taskbar at the bottom of the screen)

3 The app is added to the Start Menu (or Taskbar), from where it can be moved and resized (see pages 21-22)

Apps can be unpinned from the Start Menu (or Taskbar) by right-clicking on them and selecting **Unpin from Start** from the menu that appears.

Moving Tiles

Once apps have been added to the Start Menu, their tiles can be moved around as required. By default, tiles are displayed in groups. Apps can be moved within a group and also added to, or removed from groups:

1 Click and hold on the app's tile that you want to move

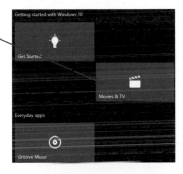

2 Drag the app's tile into its new position

3 Drag the title bar of a group of apps to move and reposition the whole group at the same time

Drag on a group name to move the whole group. If a group is moved on the Start Menu, its name moves with it.

Hot tip

Resizing Tiles

One of the advantages of using tiles on the Start Menu is that you can customize them to your own style, in terms of their size and type. One of the options for this is to resize the tiles, which is useful for the ones you use most frequently and also for live tiles, which display real-time information from the app itself. Live tiles can be more effective with larger tiles. To resize tiles on the Start Menu:

1 Right-click on a tile and click on the **Resize** button

2 Click on one of the Resize options. These are **Small**, **Medium**, **Wide** or **Large**

3 Depending on the selection in Step 2, the other tiles will move accordingly to accommodate the size of the new tile

4 Tiles can be resized in a variety of ways to give you exactly the Start Menu arrangement that you want

Using Live Tiles

The tiles on the Start Menu can be used to display real-time information from their respective apps. For instance, you can use the Photos app to show a slideshow of the photos within it, or the News app to show the latest news updates from the web service that provides this (usually Bing). To use live tiles:

1 If a live tile is on, the information from the app is displayed on the tile, rather than just a colored block

2 To turn on a live tile, right-click on the tile and click on the **Turn live tile on** button

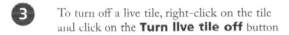

3 To turn off a live tile, right-click on the tile and click on the **Turn live tile off** button

4 The app reverts to a colored tile

Naming Groups

Groups on the Start Menu can be named and renamed:

1 For a new group, click on the title bar

2 Click on the group name so that it is highlighted

Everyday apps

3 Enter the new name for the group

My best apps

4 The new group name appears on the title bar, above the group's apps

Group names can be edited with the same process as when first creating them.

3 Getting Around

This chapter covers all of the essential functionality of Windows 10, so you can quickly get up and running with the new Windows operating system. It shows how to navigate the Desktop and Taskbar, use the new Task View feature to access your open apps, add more Desktops if required, search for items with text searches or the new voice search function, Cortana, and set up and view your Notifications.

The Desktop

When Windows 8 was introduced there was a certain amount of consternation among users, in that the traditional Desktop did not appear by default when the computer was turned on. This has been addressed in Windows 10 so that desktop computers and laptops with a mouse and keyboard open at the Desktop.

The Desktop is the area where shortcuts can be added so that apps, documents, folders and locations can be opened quickly. At the bottom of the Desktop is the Start Button and the Taskbar.

1 From any open window the Desktop can be accessed by clicking here at the right-hand side of the Taskbar

Don't forget

The Desktop can also be accessed from any open window by right-clicking on the Start Button and selecting **Desktop**.

Adding Items to the Desktop

Shortcut icons can be added to the Desktop in a number of ways:

1 Open File Explorer (from the Start Menu or Taskbar)

2 Right-click on an item such as a file, folder or app and click on the **Create shortcut** button, to create a shortcut in the same location

3 Drag the shortcut onto the Desktop to add it here, or

 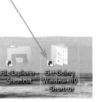

4 Click on the **Start Button**

5 Drag an item from the Start Menu, or the **All apps** section, onto the Desktop to create the shortcut

Shortcuts on the Desktop can be renamed by right-clicking on them and clicking on the **Rename** button.

Using the Taskbar

The Taskbar is located at the bottom of the Windows 10 screen. By default, it appears regardless of whichever other apps are being used or viewed. The Taskbar consists of a number of items:

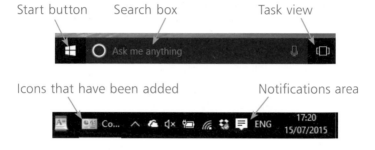

Start button   Search box   Task view

Icons that have been added   Notifications area

Adding items to the Taskbar

The icons for the apps you use most frequently can be added to the Taskbar, for quick access. To do this:

1. Click on the **Start Button**

2. Click on the **All apps** button

3. Right-click on an app and click on the **Pin to taskbar** button

   Calendar

   Camera

   Unpin from Start

   Pin to taskbar

4. The app's icon is added to the Taskbar. Click on it once to open the app

Working with the Taskbar

There are a number of options for working with the Taskbar:

1 Right-click on a space on the Taskbar and click on the **Lock the taskbar** button. This will keep it visible regardless of whatever else is on the screen

2 Right-click on a space on the Taskbar and click on the **Properties** button

3 Check On or Off the **Auto-hide the taskbar** option. If it is On, the Taskbar will disappear until you move the cursor over the bottom of the screen

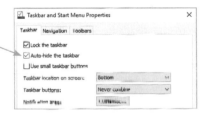

4 Click here to select whether the Taskbar appears at the **Bottom**, **Left**, **Right** or **Top** of the screen

Task View

A new feature in Windows 10 is the Task View option. This is located on the Taskbar and can be used to view all open windows and also add new desktops. To use Task View:

1 Click on this button on the Taskbar

2 To show or hide the Task View button, right-click on the button and check On or Off the **Show Task View button** option

3 The Task View displays minimized versions of the currently open windows

From any active window, press Alt + Tab to view all of the open windows. Press Tab to scroll through them.

4   As more windows are opened, the format is arranged
    accordingly

5   If an app has more than one window open, e.g. File Explorer,
    each window is displayed within Task View

6   Click on a window in Task View to make it the active window

Creating Additional Desktops

Another function within Task View is for creating additional desktops. This can be useful if you want to keep different categories of tasks on your computer separate. For instance, you may want to keep your open entertainment apps on a separate desktop from your productivity ones. To create additional desktops:

1 Click on the **Task View** button on the Taskbar

2 The current desktop is displayed, with the open windows

3 Click on the **New desktop** button

4 The new desktop is displayed at the bottom of the Task View window

Apps can only be open on one desktop at a time. So if an app is open on one desktop and you try to open it on another, you will be taken to the already-open app.

5 Click on the new desktop button to access it. Each desktop has the same background and shortcuts

6 Open apps on the new desktop. These will be separate from the apps on any other desktop

7 Click on the **Task View** button to move between desktops

Although the shortcuts and background are the same for each desktop, the Taskbar will change depending on the open apps.

33

Searching

Searching for items and information on computers and the internet has come a long way since the first search engines on the web. Most computer operating systems have sophisticated search facilities for finding things on your own computer and also searching over the web. They also now have personal digital assistants (PDAs), which are voice activated search options, which can be used instead of typing search requests.

Windows 10 has a search box built in to the Taskbar, which also includes the personal digital assistant, Cortana. This can be used for a wide range of voice activated tasks.

Using the Search box for text searching

To use the Search box for text-only searches, over either your computer or the web:

1 Click in the Search box

2 Enter a search term (or website address)

3 Click on one of the results, or on the **Web** button, to view the search results in the Windows Edge browser

...cont'd

Asking a question

The Search box can also be used to ask specific questions:

1   Enter a question in the Search box

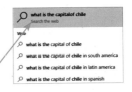

2   Click on the **Search the web** button at the top of the search box to view the results in the Windows Edge browser

Searching over your computer

As well as searching over the web, the Search box can also be used to find items on your computer:

1   Enter a search query into the search box and click on the **My stuff** button

2   Click on one of the results to open the item on your computer

Cortana

To ensure that you can use Cortana to perform voice searches and queries, the language settings on your Windows 10 computer have to be set up correctly. To do this:

1 Open the **Settings** app and click on the **Time & language** button

Time & language
Speech, region, date

2 Click on the **Region & language** button

Region & language

3 Click here to select a country or region

Country or region

Windows and apps might use your country or region to give you local content

United Kingdom

4 Click on the required display language and click on the **Set as default** button

Languages

Add a language to read and type in that language

+ Add a language

English (United States)
Will be display language after next sign-in

English (United Kingdom)
Windows display language

Set as default   Options   Remove

5 Click on the **Speech** button under **Time & language**

Speech

6 Select the same **Speech language** as the one used as the display language in Step 4

Speech language

Choose the language you speak to your device

English (United Kingdom) ∨

Setting up the microphone
To set up your computer's microphone:

1 Open the **Settings** app and click on the **Time & language** button

2 Click on the **Speech** button

3 Under the **Microphone** section, click on the **Get started** button

4 In the microphone wizard, click on **Next**

5 Repeat the phrase in the wizard window to complete setting up your microphone. (If the setup is successful the wizard will move to the completion page automatically)

6 Click on the **Finish** button <u>F</u>inish

…cont'd

Searching with Cortana

As with text searches, Cortana can be used to search over various locations and for different items:

1 Click on the microphone button in the Search box to begin a voice search

2 The Cortana symbol is displayed in the Search window with the word **Listening** in the Search box. Say what you want to find

3 Cortana can be used to open specific apps, e.g. by saying **"Open Mail"**

4 If the query is general, e.g. **Open Microsoft**, various options will be displayed. For a specific request, e.g. **Open Microsoft Edge**, the required app will be opened

Cortana Settings

Settings for Cortana can be accessed from the Search window:

1 Click in the Search box, click on this button (**Notebook**) and click on the **Settings** button

Notebook

A☰ About Me

⊞ Connected Accounts

⚙ Settings

2 Apply the Cortana Settings as required, including an option for Cortana to provide its own suggestions and also setting Cortana to respond to saying "**Hey Cortana**" from any screen or app

Settings

Cortana can give you suggestions, ideas, reminders, alerts and more.

On

Turning Cortana off clears what Cortana knows on this device, but won't delete anything from the Notebook. Once Cortana is off, you can decide what you'd like to do with anything still stored in the cloud.

Manage what Cortana knows about me in the cloud

Hey Cortana
Let Cortana respond to "Hey Cortana."

Off

Cortana is always ready when this is on, which uses more battery.

Find flights and more
Detect tracking info, such as flights, in messages on my device.

On

3 Scroll up the Settings window to access more options

Taskbar tidbits
Let Cortana pipe up from time to time with thoughts and greetings in the Search box.

On

Bing SafeSearch settings
Change how Bing filters adult content from your search results.

Other privacy settings
See the Privacy Statement or manage other personal information settings.

Learn more about Cortana & Search

Reminders

The Cortana Search box can also be used to set reminders, that appear when required. To do this:

1. Click in the Search box and click on this button in the side toolbar

Reminders
⌂ **All** Time Place Person
▣ Select + to add a new reminder
♀
₰

2. Select from the top toolbar whether the reminder is for a **Time**, **Place**, **Person** or **All** (the default option)

3. Click on this button to add a new reminder

≡ + ⋯

4. Click in the **Remember to...** text box to add the item for which you want the reminder

5. Enter the reminder item

What do you want to be reminded about?

Reminder

Take suit to drycleaners

Person, Place or Time

Remind   Cancel

6 Click in the **Time** text box to set a time for the reminder. Click here to apply the time

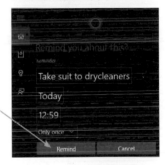

7 Enter any other criteria for the reminder and click on the **Remind** button

8 The details of the reminder are confirmed

9 When it is time for the reminder, it pops up from the Notifications area on the Taskbar and also appears in the Cortana window

Working with Notifications

In the modern digital world there is an increasing desire to keep updated with what is happening in our online world. With Windows 10, the Notifications panel can be used to display information from a variety of sources, so that you never miss an update or a notification from one of your apps. To view your notifications:

1 Click on the **Notifications** button on the Taskbar

2 New notifications appear at the top of the panel. Click on an item to access it directly, within its own app (the Notifications panel is also known as the Action Center)

3 Quick action buttons appear at the bottom of the panel. Click on an item to activate or deactivate it (when a button is blue, the item is active)

To apply settings for the Notifications panel: Click on the **Settings** app and access **System > Notifications & actions** and drag the buttons **On** or **Off** for items to appear on the Notifications panel.

④ Settings

Most users like to customize their computer so that it has its own look and feel. With Windows 10 there are numerous settings that can be applied to improve the functionality of Windows 10 for what you need, and also personalization options so that you can change its overall appearance. This chapter details all of the settings available with Windows 10 so that you can have as much control over the operating system as possible.

Accessing Settings

The Settings in Windows 10 provide options for how you set up your computer and how it operates. There are nine main categories of Settings, each of which have a number of sub-categories. The Settings app can be accessed in a number of ways:

1 Click on the **Start Button**

2 Click on the **Settings** button on the Start Menu or the **Settings** tile on the Start Menu, or

3 Click on the **Notifications** button on the Taskbar

4 Click on the **All settings** button

5 In the **Settings** app, click on one of the main categories to view the options within that category

System Settings

The System Settings provide numerous options to specify how your computer looks and operates. They include:

- **Display**. This contains options for changing the size of items on the screen, the orientation of the screen and options for adjusting the screen brightness, either manually or automatically.

- **Notifications & actions**. This contains options for selecting which Notification icons appear on the Taskbar and specifying which apps can be used to display notifications, e.g. Calendar and Mail.

- **Apps & features**. This contains information about the apps that you have on your computer. This includes their size and installation date. Click on an app and click on the **Uninstall** button to remove it.

- **Multitasking**. This contains options for working with windows and desktops. In the **Snap** section you can turn on options for arranging windows when they are moved to the edge of the screen and in the **Virtual desktops** sections you can specify whether the Taskbar (and Alt + Tab) shows all open windows, or just those for the current desktop.

...cont'd

- **Tablet mode**. This can be used on desktop and laptop computers using a mouse and keyboard to replicate the operation of using a touchscreen device or tablet with Windows 10. This includes expanding the Start Menu to full screen.

- **Battery saver**. This can be used on laptops, and displays the charge level of the battery and what is using the most power. It also has options for saving battery power.

- **Power & sleep**. This contains options for when the screen turns off when not being used, and when the computer goes to sleep when it is not being used. This ranges from one minute to never.

- **Storage**. This displays how much storage has been taken up on your computer and has options for where you want to save certain types of content. This can be on the PC or an external drive.

- **Offline maps**. This contains options for downloading maps so that you can use them even when you are offline. There is also an option for only downloading maps when you are connected to Wi-Fi, to save any unwanted charges if you have a mobile data plan.

- **Default apps**. This contains options for selecting default apps that open for specific tasks, such as for web browsing, playing music or viewing photos.

- **About**. This contains information about your computer and the version of Windows that you are using.

Devices Settings

The Devices Settings provide settings for how the hardware connected with your computer operates. They include:

- **Printers & scanners**. This can be used to add new printers or scanners to your computer. These can either be wireless devices or ones which connect via cable. In most cases, the required software will be installed with Windows 10 or, if not, it will be downloaded from the internet.

- **Connected devices**. This can be used to add new devices, such as a printer, using the **Add a device** button.

- **Bluetooth**. This can be used to link your computer to compatible Bluetooth devices, so that they can share content over short distances with radiowaves. The two devices have to be "paired" initially to be able to share content.

- **Mouse & touchpad**. This contains options for customizing the mouse and touchpad (for a laptop). These include setting the main button on the mouse (Left, by default) and how the scrolling operates with the mouse, such as the number of lines that can be scrolled at a time (Multiple, by default).

- **Typing**. This contains options for correcting your typing as you go. These include auto-correcting misspelt words and highlighting misspelt words.

- **AutoPlay**. This contains options for applying AutoPlay for external devices such as removable drives and memory cards. If AutoPlay is On, the devices will be activated and accessed when they are attached to your computer.

Network & Internet Settings

The Network & Internet Settings provide settings related to connecting to networks, usually for accessing the internet. They include:

- **Wi-Fi**. This contains options for connecting to the internet via your Wi-Fi router (or a public hotspot if you are away from home). There is also an option for managing your Wi-Fi networks.

- **Airplane mode**. This can be used to turn off wireless communication when you are on a plane, so that you can still use your computer (laptop) safely.

- **Data usage**. This displays how much data has been downloaded over any networks that you are using. The most common one is Wi-Fi and displays your usage over a 30-day period.

- **VPN**. This can be used to connect to a corporate network over VPN (Virtual Private Network). If you are doing this, you will need certain settings from your network administrator.

- **Dial-up**. This can be used if you have a dial-up modem for connecting to the internet. This is not common these days, but it is still a valid means of internet access.

- **Ethernet**. This can be used if you are connecting to the internet with an Ethernet cable. This connects to the Ethernet port on your computer, and internet access is delivered through your telephone line.

- **Proxy**. This contains options for using a proxy server for Ethernet or Wi-Fi connections.

Personalization Settings

The Personalization Settings provide options for customizing the look and feel of Windows 10. They include:

- **Background**. This can be used to change the Desktop background in Windows 10. You can select images from the pictures provided, solid colors, or a slideshow of your own photos (or browse to select a single one using the **Browse** button). You can also choose how the background fits the screen (the default is for Fill).

- **Colors**. This contains options for selecting a color for borders, buttons, the Taskbar and the Start Menu background.

- **Lock screen**. This can be used to select a background for the Lock Screen. You can use the images provided and also select your own photos (using the **Browse** button). You can also select apps that display relevant information on the Lock Screen, such as email notifications or calendar events.

- **Themes**. This contains a link to the Control Panel, where color themes can be applied for several elements within the Windows 10 interface.

- **Start**. This contains options for how the Start Menu operates. It can be used to display the Start Menu in full-screen mode and also show recently used items in the Start Menu and on the Taskbar.

Accounts Settings

The Accounts Settings provide options for adding new online accounts (such as a new email account, or an online storage and sharing service such as Dropbox). They include:

- **Your account**. This displays information about your current account, which will either be the one you signed in with using your Microsoft Account details, or a local account, which has no online presence. You can also swap between accounts here.

- **Sign-in options**. This contains security options for signing in to your account. You can create a PIN, password or picture password. Whichever method you choose, this will be required to sign in to your account from the Lock screen.

- **Work access**. This can be used to connect to a workplace network, where you can share certain items. To do this you will need to contact the network administrator in order to obtain the correct settings to connect to the network.

- **Family & other users**. This can be used to set up accounts on your computer for other family members, or friends. They will be able to set their own sign-in options and you will be able to switch users by clicking on the Start button and then clicking on the icon of the current user.

- **Sync your settings**. This can be used to sync the settings you have on your computer with any other Windows 10 devices that you have. For instance, if you have a desktop computer using Windows 10, you will be able to sync settings and apps with another Windows 10 device such as a Surface tablet.

Time & Language Settings

The Time & Language Settings provide options for the time zone used by your computer and the format for these items. They include:

- **Date & time**. This can be used to set the date and time, either manually, or automatically, using the **Time zone** drop-down menu. There is also a link to **Related settings** in the Control Panel, where formatting options can be applied.

- **Region & language**. This can be used to select the language that is used by your computer, e.g. English (United States). You can also add new languages.

- **Speech**. This contains options for how the speech function operates when using Windows 10. This includes the language to use when you are using speech, and also the default voice if using apps that speak text from the screen.

The language in **Region & language** and **Speech** must be set to the same in order for the digital assistant, Cortana, to work.

Settings

Ease of Access Settings

The Ease of Access Settings contain a range of options to help users who have visual or motor issues when using a computer. They include:

- **Narrator**. This can be used to turn on a screen reader so text, buttons and toolbars can be read out loud. You can choose a voice style for the narrator and the speed and pitch of reading.

- **Magnifier**. This can be used to magnify what is being viewed on the screen. The amount of magnification can be increased up to 1600% of the standard view. The color of the screen can also be inverted.

- **High contrast**. This contains options for applying high contrast themes for Windows 10, to make certain elements more pronounced. This can be useful for users with dyslexia.

- **Closed captions**. This can be used by hearing-impaired users to provide text subtitles for items such as movies or multimedia content. The captioning is included in the media, and the settings enable you to select color, size and effects for the subtitles.

- **Keyboard**. This can be used to enable the on-screen keyboard and options for keyboard shortcuts and sounds for when certain keys are pressed, e.g. Caps Lock and Number Lock.

- **Mouse**. This contains options for setting the size of the mouse pointer and also its color.

- **Other options**. This contains options for turning off animations and Windows backgrounds, to make the screen less distracting, and also options for showing notifications.

Privacy Settings

The Privacy Settings can be used for a range of settings for your personal information and also for allowing, or denying, certain apps access to your location, but you may want to restrict this for some apps. They include:

- **General** – for allowing, or denying, apps access to some of your personal information (such as name, picture and account info), using a SmartScreen Filter to check web pages used by certain apps, send Microsoft information about your typing, and allowing websites to provide you with local information.

- **Location** – for turning On or Off the location services, to allow, or deny, apps the use of your current location.

- The following options can be used to allow, or deny, apps access to these specific apps: **Camera**, **Microphone**, **Contacts**, **Calendar**, **Messaging**, and **Radios**.

- **Speech, inking & typing** – for training Windows and the digital assistant, Cortana, to get to know your writing and speaking styles.

- **Account info** – for allowing apps access to your name, picture and account info.

- **Other devices** – used to view external devices, such as an Xbox, which have access to your apps.

- **Feedback & diagnostics** – contains options for how feedback is asked for by Microsoft.

- **Background apps** – used to specify which apps can receive notifications and updates even when not in use. This includes Mail and the Microsoft Edge browser.

Update & Security Settings

The Update & Security Settings provide options for installing updates to Windows and also backing up and recovering the data on your computer. They include:

- **Windows Update**. This can be used to install system updates, such as those to Windows 10 and also important security updates. They can be set to be checked for and installed automatically (using the **Advanced options** button) or manually using the **Check for updates** button. For some updates, your computer will shut down and restart automatically.

- **Windows Defender**. This contains options for protecting your computer with the Windows Defender app, including real-time protection and protection for items stored in the cloud.

- **Backup**. This can be used to back up your important files and documents. It is best if this is done to an external hard drive that is kept separately from your computer.

- **Recovery**. This can be used if you encounter problems with the way that Windows 10 is operating. You can select to refresh your computer and keep all of your files intact (although they should always be backed up first); reinstall Windows completely, which will reset it completely and you will lose all of your files and any apps you have downloaded; or return to an earlier version of Windows that was on your computer, without losing any files.

- **Activation.** This can be used to activate your copy of Windows 10 online, to confirm that it is an authorized version.

- **For developers**. This contains options for advanced users involved in programming and app development.

5 Windows Apps

Apps, or computer programs, are the lifeblood of Windows 10, as they are used to undertake almost all of the tasks on your computer. In Windows 10, some apps are pre-installed, as with previous versions of Windows, while hundreds more can be downloaded from the Windows Store. This chapter shows how to work with and organize apps in Windows 10 and how to find your way around the Windows Store.

About Windows Apps

There are three types of apps within Windows 10:

- **New Windows 10 apps**. These are the built-in apps that appear on the Start Menu. They cover the areas of communication, entertainment and information and several of them are linked together through the online sharing service, OneDrive.

- **Windows classic apps**. These are the old-style Windows apps that people may be familiar with from previous versions of Windows. These open in the Desktop environment.

- **Windows Store apps**. These are apps that can be downloaded from the online Windows Store, and cover a wide range of subjects and functionality. Some Windows Store apps are free, while others have to be paid for.

New Windows 10 apps

Windows 10 apps are generally those which appear with the colored tiles on the Start Menu. They can also be accessed from the **All apps** button on the Start Menu. In Windows 10, these apps open on the Desktop, in a similar way as the older style of Windows apps.

Windows classic apps

The Windows classic apps are generally the ones that appeared as default with previous versions of Windows (pre-Windows 8). The Windows apps can be accessed from the Start Menu by clicking on the **All apps** button. Older style Windows apps can also be pinned to the Start Menu and Taskbar in the same way as for Windows 10 apps.

Windows Store apps

The Windows Store apps are accessed and downloaded from the online Windows Store. Apps can be browsed and searched for in the Store, and when they are downloaded they are added to the All Apps section of the Start Menu.

Built-in Windows Apps

The Windows 10 apps that are accessed from the **All apps** button on the Start Menu cover a range of communication, entertainment and information functions. The apps include:

Alarms & Clock. This provides alarms, clocks for times around the world, a timer and a stopwatch function.

Calculator. This is a standard calculator that also has an option for using it as a scientific calculator.

Calendar. This is a calendar which you can use to add appointments and important dates.

Camera. This can be used to take photos directly onto your computer, but only if it has a built-in camera.

Food & Drink. This contains recipes from top chefs, options for adding shopping lists, and meal planning.

Fresh Paint. An app for creating your own artwork and also viewing photos.

Groove Music. This can be used to access the online Music section of the Windows Store, where music can be downloaded.

Health & Fitness. This contains options for monitoring your diet and exercise regime.

Traditional Windows apps, such as Notepad and Paint, can be found under **Windows Accessories** from the **All apps** button on the **Start Menu**.

Mail. This is the online Mail facility. You can use it to connect to a selection of email accounts. Several accounts can be added so that you can access all of your emails here.

Maps. This provides online and offline access to maps from around the world. It also shows traffic issues.

Microsoft Edge. This is the new default browser in Windows 10, replacing Internet Explorer (although Internet Explorer can still be used, if required).

Money. This is one of the information apps that provides real-time financial news. This is based on your location as entered when you installed Windows 10.

Movies & TV. This can be used to access the online Movies & TV section of the Windows Store, where movies and TV shows can be downloaded.

News. This is one of the information apps that provides real-time news information. This is based on your location as entered at installation.

OneDrive. This is an online facility for storing and sharing content from your computer. This includes photos and documents.

OneNote. This is the Microsoft note-taking app; part of the Office suite of apps.

People. This is the address book app for adding contacts. Your contacts from sites such as Facebook and Twitter can also be imported into the People app.

Photos. This can be used to view and organize your photos. You can also share and print photos directly from the Photos app.

Reader. This can be used to open and view documents in different file formats, such as PDF and TIFF.

Reading List. This can be used to save web pages for reading at a later time, even when you are offline.

Settings. This can be used to access all of the main settings for customizing and managing Windows 10 and your computer.

Sport. This is one of the information apps that provide real-time sports news. This is based on your location as entered when you installed Windows 10.

Store. This provides access to the online Windows Store, from where a range of other apps can be bought and downloaded to your computer.

Weather. This provides real-time weather forecasts for locations around the world. By default, it will provide the nearest forecast to your location as entered when you installed Windows 10.

Xbox. This can be used to download and play games and also play online Xbox games. This can be done with standalone games or with other people in multi-player games.

Don't forget

The information for the Money, News, Sports and Weather apps is provided by the Bing search engine.

Navigating Apps

In Windows 8, the newer Windows apps operated in a slightly different way to the more traditional ones, in that they only opened in full-screen. However, in Windows 10, the operation of all apps has been standardized:

1 Apps open in their own windows which appear on the Desktop

2 Click on this button to maximize an app to full-screen (or double-click in the middle of the top bar)

3 Click on this button to minimize an app to its own window (or double-click in the middle of the top bar)

4 Click on this button to minimize an app onto the Taskbar

5 Click on this button to close an app

6 Some of the newer Windows apps have their own menu button within the app. Click on this button (if it is available) to access an app's menu options, which usually include its settings

Accessing Apps

There is a lot more to Windows 10 than the default Windows 10 apps. Most of the Windows apps that were available with previous versions of Windows are still there, just not initially visible on the Start Menu. However, it only takes two clicks on the Start Menu to view all of the apps on your computer.

1 Click on the **Start Button**

2 Click on the **All apps** button

3 All of the apps are displayed. Use the scroll bar to move through all of the apps

4 Click on a letter heading to view an alphabetic grid for finding apps. Click on a letter to move to that section

5 Click on the **Back** button to go back to the full list of apps

6 When new apps are added, e.g. downloaded from the Windows Store, this is noted next to the **All apps** button

Using the Windows Store

The third category of apps that can be used with Windows 10 are those that are downloaded from the Windows Store. These cover a wide range of topics and provide an excellent way to add functionality to Windows 10. To use the Windows Store:

1   Click or tap on the **Store** tile on the Start Menu

2   The currently-featured apps are displayed on the Homepage

3   Scroll down to see additional featured apps

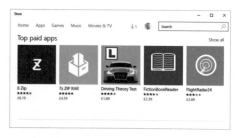

4 Click on the **App top charts** button on the Homepage and select apps under specific headings, e.g. **Best rated** apps

App top charts

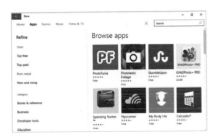

5 Click on options in the **Refine** section to view apps according to certain criteria, e.g. **Top free**

6 Click on an app to preview it

Finding Apps

To find more apps in the Windows Store:

1   Click on the **App categories** button at the top of the Homepage, to view the available categories

App categories

2   Click on a category to access it

3   Click on items in each category to view details about them. Click on the Back arrow to go back up one level each time

4   Enter a word or phrase into the search box to see matching apps. Click on a result to view the app

Downloading Apps

When you find an app that you want to use, you can download it to your computer or tablet. To do this:

1 Access the app and click on the **Free (or price)** button

2 The app downloads from the Windows Store. Click on the **Install** button to install the downloaded app

3 The app is added to the All apps page and has a **New** tag next to it. This disappears once the app has been opened

4 Click on the app to open it and use it. (It can also be pinned to the Start Menu or the Taskbar.)

If there is a fee for an app, this will be displayed on, or next to, the **Install** button.

Uninstalling Apps

In Windows 10, apps can be uninstalled from the Control Panel and also directly from the Start Menu. To do this:

1 Right-click on an app and click on the **Uninstall** button

2 A window alerts you to the fact that related information will be removed if the app is uninstalled. Click or tap on the **Uninstall** button if you want to continue

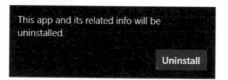

3 If the app is a new Windows 10 one, or has been pinned to the Start Menu, its tile will be removed. For other apps, they will no longer be available from the All apps option

6 File Explorer

The File Explorer in Windows 10 is at the heart of working with the files on your computer and you can use it to browse all of the information on your computer and on the local network. This chapter shows how you can use the Scenic Ribbon function, modify the views in File Explorer, use the Quick Access option for files and folders that you use most frequently, and customize the style and appearance.

Around File Explorer

File Explorer plays an important role in organizing your folders and files. To access File Explorer:

1 Right-click on the Start Menu and click on the **All apps** button. Select the **File Explorer** button, or

2 Click on this icon on the Taskbar, or

3 Press **WinKey** + **E**, and File Explorer opens with the **Quick access** folder

4 When File Explorer is opened, click on the **This PC** link to view the top level items on your computer, including the main folders, your hard drive and any removable devices that are connected

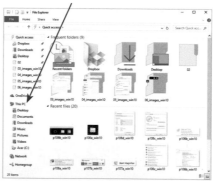

...cont'd

The elements of File Explorer consist of:

Ribbon   Menu Bar   Address Bar   Search

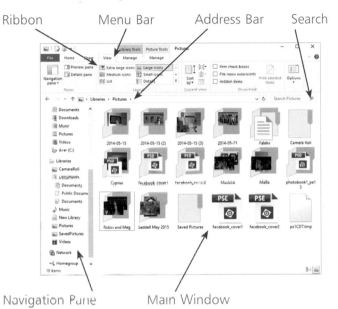

Navigation Pane   Main Window

The **View** menu on the Menu Bar can be used to display the items in the main window in different ways, such as Large icons or Details.

The **This PC** section displays files from different locations as a single collection, without actually moving any files.

File Explorer Libraries

File Explorer can use the Library for accessing files and folders on
your computer and network. Each Library displays files from several
locations. Initially, there are five Libraries defined:

- **Camera Roll**, which is the default folder for photos captured on
  your computer (if it has a camera attached).

- **Documents**, which is the default folder for files such as those
  created with word processing or presentation apps.

- **Music**, which is the default folder for music bought from the
  online Windows Store, or added yourself.

- **Pictures**, which is the default folder for your photos.

- **Videos**, which is the default folder for your videos.

To view the Pictures Library, for
example:

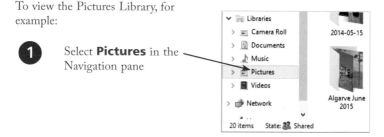

1 Select **Pictures** in the
Navigation pane

If the main **Libraries** folder is not
displayed, click on the **Navigation pane**
button (see Step 4 on page 74) and click on
the **Show libraries** button.

…cont'd

To add another folder to a Library:

1 Right-click in the Library window and select **New > Folder**

2 Click on the folder name and overwrite it with a new title

New libraries can also be created, by right-clicking on the Libraries folder in the Navigation pane and selecting **New > Library** from the menu.

Navigation Panes

The normal view for File Explorer includes the Navigation pane. There is also a Preview pane and a Details pane available.

You can choose different panes to display:

1 Open File Explorer and click on the **View** button. This will open the Ribbon

2 The Pane options are located at the left-hand side of the Ribbon

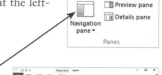

3 Click on the **Navigation pane** button to view this format. This appears down the left-hand side

4 Click on the arrow on the **Navigation pane** button and click here to show or hide the Navigation pane. There are also options here for showing all folders and libraries

5 Click on the **Preview pane** button to view a preview of the folder or file selected in the main window

6 Click on the **Details pane** button to view additional information about the folder or file selected in the main window

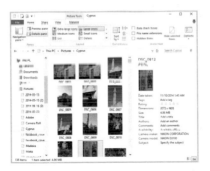

Quick Access

When working with files and folders there will probably be items which you access on a regular basis. The Quick access section of File Explorer can be used to view the items that you have most recently accessed, and also pin your most frequently used and favorite items. To use the Quick access section:

1 Click on the **Quick access** button in the File Explorer Navigation pane

> ✓ ⭐ Quick access
> \> ⭐ Quick access

2 In the main window, your frequently-used folders and most recently-used files are displayed

3 The folders are also listed underneath the **Quick access** button in the navigation pane

Adding items to Quick access

The folders that you access and use most frequently can be pinned to the Quick access section. This does not physically move them; it just creates a shortcut within Quick access. To do this:

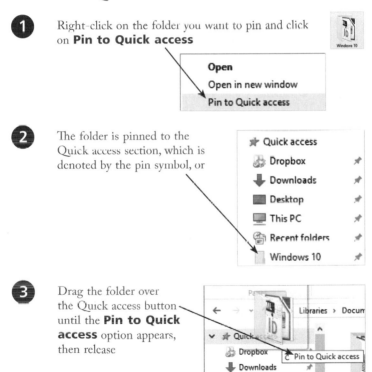

1 Right-click on the folder you want to pin and click on **Pin to Quick access**

> Open
> Open in new window
> Pin to Quick access

2 The folder is pinned to the Quick access section, which is denoted by the pin symbol, or

> ★ Quick access
> 🗂 Dropbox
> ⬇ Downloads
> ▪ Desktop
> 🖥 This PC
> 🗂 Recent folders
> Windows 10

3 Drag the folder over the Quick access button until the **Pin to Quick access** option appears, then release

> ← → ∨ Libraries › Docum
> ∨ ★ Quick access
> 🗂 Dropbox   Pin to Quick access
> ⬇ Downloads
> ▪ Desktop

Using the Ribbon

The navigation and functionality in the Libraries is done by the Scenic Ribbon at the top of the window. This has options for the Library itself and also the type of content that is being viewed.

1 Click on the tabs at the top of the Library window to view associated tools

2 Click on the **Library Tools** tab to view the menus for the whole Library (see below)

3 Click on the content tab (**Picture Tools** in this example) to view menus for the selected content

Library File Menu

This contains options for opening a new window, closing the current window or moving to a frequently-visited location in the Library.

Library Home Menu

This contains options for copying and pasting, moving, deleting and

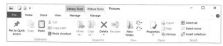

renaming selected items. You can also create new folders, view folder properties and select all items in a folder.

View Options

You can change the size and appearance of the file and folder icons in your folders, using the View tab on the Scenic Ribbon.

1 Open the folder you would like to change and click on the **View** tab on the Ribbon. Select one of the options for viewing content in the folder

2 Click on different items to change the appearance of icons

3 Pause at any position, holding the mouse button, to see the effect. Release the mouse button to apply that view

Exploring Drives

Explore the contents of any drive from the **This PC** folder.

1 Select one of the drive icons – for example, the **Pen Drive** removable storage device

2 Double-click the **Pen Drive** device icon (or select it and press **Enter**) to display the files and folders that it contains

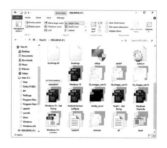

3 Double-click a folder entry (e.g. Windows 10) and select one of the files

4 Double-click the file icon (or select it and press **Enter**) to open the file using the associated application, e.g. Paint

File Explorer Address Bar

The Address bar at the top of File Explorer displays the current location as a set of names separated by arrows, and offers another way to navigate between libraries and locations.

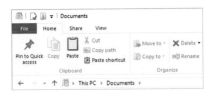

1 To go to a location that is named in the address, click on that name in the Address bar, e.g. Documents

2 To select a subfolder of a library or location named in the Address bar, click on the arrow to the right

3 Click one of the entries to open it in place of the current location

When you are viewing a drive rather than a library, the Address bar shows the drive and its folders, and allows you to navigate amongst these.

Folder Options

You can change the appearance and the behavior of your folders by adjusting the folder settings.

1 From the View tab in the Ribbon, click on the **Options** button and select the **Change folder and search options** link

2 Choose **Open each folder in its own window**, to keep multiple folders open at the same time

3 If you want items to open as they do on a web page, select **Single-click to open an item (point to select)**

4 Select the **View** tab to select options for how items appear in File Explorer libraries

5 Select **Apply** to try out the selected changes without closing the Folder Options

Apply

6 Select **Restore Defaults** then **Apply**, to reset all options to their default values

Restore Defaults

7 OneDrive

OneDrive is Microsoft's online "cloud" storage and backup facility. It can be used to manually or automatically back up your files and documents and store them safely away from your computer, while still making them available on your devices, or online. This chapter shows how to set up OneDrive with Windows 10, and details how to add files to it once it has been set up.

Setting Up OneDrive

Cloud computing is now a mainstream part of our online experience. This involves saving content to an online server connected to the service that you are using, i.e. through your Microsoft Account. You can then access this content from any computer, using your account login details, and also share it with other people by giving them access to your cloud service. It can also be used to back up your files, in case they are corrupted or damaged on your PC.

The cloud service for Windows 10 is known as OneDrive and you can use it providing that you have a Microsoft Account.

1 Click on the **OneDrive** tile on the Start Menu

2 Click on the **Get started** button

3 Sign in with your Microsoft Account details

Microsoft OneDrive — □ ×

Welcome to OneDrive

Your most important files are with you wherever you go, on any device.

Get started

By default, you get 15GB of free OneDrive storage space with Windows 10 (*correct at the time of printing*). This is an excellent way to back up your important documents.

4 Select the folder that you want to sync to OneDrive and click on the **Next** button

Next

5 The OneDrive folders are displayed within File Explorer

6 Click on one of the folders to view its contents

Using OneDrive Online

OneDrive is an online service and this enables you to access and manage your files from any web browser with an active internet connection. To do this:

1 Go to the website at **OneDrive.live.com** and sign in with your Microsoft Account details

2 Your OneDrive content is the same as in your OneDrive folder on your computer. Click on items to open and edit them

3 Click on the **Create** button for options for creating new documents. These will also be available from your OneDrive folder on your computer

Adding Files to OneDrive

OneDrive is built into the file structure of Windows 10 and as well as adding files from OneDrive itself, it is also possible to add them to the OneDrive folder from your computer. Once this has been done, the files can be accessed from OneDrive on your computer, online or any compatible device, using your Microsoft Account login details.

Adding from File Explorer
To add files from File Explorer:

1 In File Explorer, the OneDrive folder is located underneath Quick access

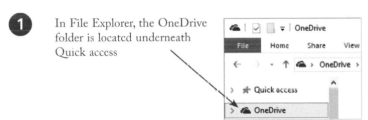

2 Click on the OneDrive folder to view its contents

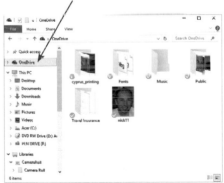

...cont'd

3 Add files to the OneDrive folder by dragging and dropping them from another folder or by using Copy and Paste

4 The new content is available from the OneDrive app and also online from your OneDrive account

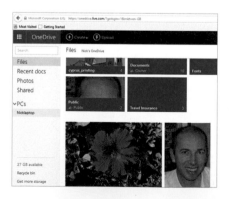

Saving files to OneDrive

Files can also be saved directly to OneDrive when they are created.
To do this:

1 Open a new file in any app
and create the required
content

2 Select **File > Save** from
the menu bar and select a
OneDrive folder into which
you want to save the file

3 Click on the **Save** button

4 The file is saved into the OneDrive
folder and will be available from the
OneDrive app and also online from your
OneDrive account

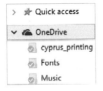

OneDrive Settings

A range of settings can be applied to OneDrive, including adding and syncing folders. To do this:

1 Right-click on the OneDrive icon on the Taskbar and click on **Settings**

2 Click on the **Settings** tab for options for starting OneDrive when you sign in and for unlinking your OneDrive so that it is not linked to the online function

3 Click on the **Choose folders** tab and click on the **Choose folders** button to select the folder from your online OneDrive that you want to sync on your computer

4 Click on the **OK** button to apply any changes to the OneDrive settings

8 To the Edge of the Web

Microsoft Edge is the latest web browser from Microsoft and is the default browser in Windows 10. It is designed as a replacement for Internet Explorer, but this is still also available. This chapter shows how to use Microsoft Edge to view web pages, use tabs and bookmarks, physically add notes to web pages, and then share them with friends and family.

Introducing Microsoft Edge

The web browser Internet Explorer (IE) has been synonymous with Microsoft for almost as long as the Windows operating system. Introduced in 1995, shortly after Windows 95, it has been the default browser for a generation of web users. However, as with most technologies, the relentless march of time has caught up with IE and, although it is still included with Windows 10, the preferred browser is a new one, designed specifically for the digital mobile age. It is called Microsoft Edge and adapts easily to whichever environment it is operating in: desktop, tablet or phone.

Microsoft Edge has a number of performance and speed enhancements from IE and it also recognizes that modern web users want a lot more from their browser than simply being able to look at web pages. It includes functions for drawing on and annotating web pages, which can then be sent to other people as screenshots.

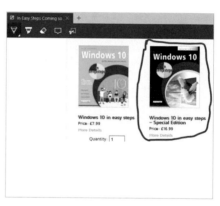

There is also a Hub where you can store all of your Favorites, downloads and pages that you have selected to read at a later date (which can be accessed when you are offline if required).

Click on this icon from the **All apps** menu or on the Taskbar to open the Microsoft Edge browser.

Smart Address Bar

Smart address bars are now a familiar feature in a lot of modern browsers and Microsoft Edge is no different. They can be used to enter a specific web address to open that page, or to search for a word or phrase. To use the Smart address bar:

1 Check anywhere in the address bar

← → ↻   🔎 ineasy|

2 Start typing a word or website address. As you type, options appear below the address bar. Click on one of the options under **Sites** to go to a specific web page

3 Click on one of the options under **Search suggestions** to go to a page with these search results

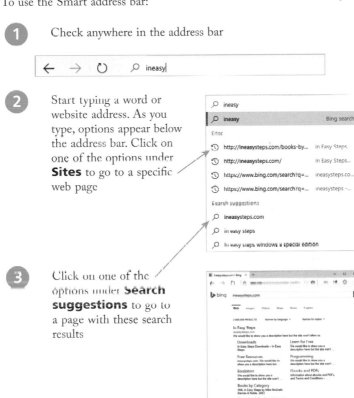

Setting a Homepage

By default, Microsoft Edge opens at its own Start page. This may not be ideal for most users, who will want to set their own Homepage to appear when Microsoft Edge is launched. To set a Homepage:

1 Click on this button on the top toolbar to access the menu options

    • • •

2 Click on the **Settings** button

    Settings

3 By default, the **Start page** is selected as the opening page

SETTINGS

Choose a theme

Light

Show the favorites bar

◯ Off

Import favorites from another browser

Open with

◉ Start page

◯ New tab page

◯ Previous pages

◯ A specific page or pages

4 Click on the **A specific page or pages** radio button

5 Click on the **Custom** button

◉ A specific page or pages

MSN

Bing

Custom

6 Enter the website address you want to use as your Homepage and click on the **+** button

ineasysteps.com   ×   +

Adding Notes to Web Pages

One of the innovations in the Microsoft Edge browser is the ability to draw on and annotate web pages. This can be useful to highlight parts of a web page or add your own comments and views, which can then be sent to other people. To add notes:

1. Open a web page to which you want to add a note or draw on, and click on this button on the toolbar of the Microsoft Edge browser

2. Click on one of the pen options

3. Click on the small triangle in the bottom right-hand corner to select formatting options and size for the pen

4. Click and drag on the web page to draw over it

...cont'd

5 Click on the eraser icon and drag over any items that you have drawn to remove them

6 Click on the text icon to add your own text

7 Drag over the web page to create a text box

> This is the one I mentioned.

> The text box appears as a note on the web page

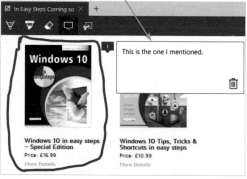

Several notes can be added to a web page, but it can begin to look a bit cluttered if there are too many.

Sharing Web Notes

Once you have created a web note (or a clipping), this can be saved or shared with other people. There is also an option for selecting part of a web page and sharing this too.

Sharing a web note
To share a web note with other people:

1 Once the web note is finished, click on this button on the toolbar to save the web note

2 Select an app into which you want to save the web note

3 The web note is displayed in the selected app

4 Click on the **Send** button to send the web note to the app

Using Tabs

Being able to open several web pages at the same time in different tabs is now a common feature of web browsers. To do this with Microsoft Edge:

1   Click on this button at the top of the Microsoft Edge window

2   Pages can be opened in new tabs using the smart address bar or the list of Top sites that appears below it. The start page for new tabs, as displayed here, can be changed, if required. (To do this, open the Microsoft Edge menu as shown on page 104 and click Settings, then change the selection under the **Open new tabs with** heading)

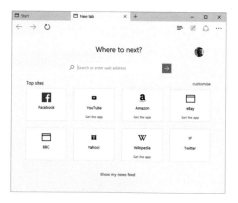

3   All open tabs are displayed at the top of the window. Click and hold on a tab to drag it into a new position

Bookmarking Web Pages

Your favorite web pages can be bookmarked so that you can access them with one click from the Hub area, rather than having to enter the web address each time. To do this:

1 Open the web page that you want to bookmark

2 Click on this button on the Microsoft Edge toolbar

3 Click on the **Favorites** button

4 Enter a name for the favorite and where you want it to be saved (click on the **Create new folder** link if you want to save it to a new location)

5 Click on the **Add** button

6 When a page has been saved as a favorite, the star in Step 2 turns yellow

7 Click on this button to access your favorites (see page 100)

Organizing with the Hub

The Hub is the area where you can store a variety of items from the Microsoft Edge browser: from your web page favorites to pages that you want to read offline at a later date. To use the Hub:

1   Click on the **Menu** button to open the Hub

2   Click on this button to view your favorites. Click on one to go to that page

3   Click on this button to view your Reading List of pages that you have saved to read offline, or at a later date

4   Click on this button to view your web browsing history

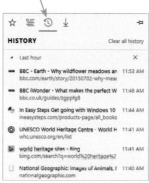

5   Click on **Clear all history** to remove all the items in the history

Clear all history

6   Click on this button to view items that you have downloaded from the web, such as PDF documents or apps to install (although not those from the Windows Store)

Reading List

With some web pages you may want to save the content so that you can read it at a later date. If you make the page a Favorite, the content could change the next time to you look at it. Instead, you can add the page to your Reading List to ensure that you can read the same content. Also, this has the advantage that you can access the items in your Reading List when you are offline and not connected to the internet. To do this:

1 Open the web page that you want to add to the Reading List

2 Click on this button on the Microsoft Edge toolbar

3 Click on the **Reading list** button

4 Enter a name for the item and click on the **Add** button

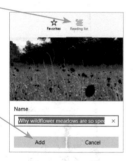

5 Click on this button within the Hub to access and view your Reading List items

Reading View

Modern web pages contain a lot more items than just text and pictures: video clips, pop-up ads, banners and more contribute to the multimedia effect on many web pages. At times, this additional content can enhance the page, but a lot of the time it is just a distraction. If you want to just concentrate on the main item on a web page you can do this with the Reading View function:

Open the web page that you want to view in Reading View

Click on this button on the Microsoft Edge toolbar

The text and pictures are presented on a new page, with any additional content removed

Click on this button to return to the standard page view

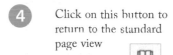

Menu Options

There is no traditional menu bar in the Microsoft Edge browser, but menu options can be accessed from the right-hand toolbar:

1 Click on this button to access the menu items

2 Click here to open a new browsing window, or a **New InPrivate window** which does not record any of your browsing history

3 Click here to increase or decrease the magnification of the page being viewed

4 Click on the **Find on page** button to search for a specific word or phrase on the web page

5 Click on the **Print** button to print the current web page

New window

New InPrivate window

Zoom   — 100% +

Find on page

Print

Pin to Start

F12 Developer Tools

Open with Internet Explorer

Send feedback

Settings

The Microsoft Edge menu also includes options to pin the current web page to the Start Menu and also open it in Internet Explorer.